Stained Glass Soldiers

Ashley Green

BookLeaf Publishing

Presentation by *BookLeaf Publishing*

Web: www.bookleafpub.com

E-mail: info@bookleafpub.com

ISBN : 9789357699495

First edition 2022

DEDICATION

For Lincoln {freedom}, King {equality}, and Zelenskyy {peace}

The black hole will never take us all, for we already live in darkness, but we are unified in light.

PREFACE

Foreword

Every poem in this book is written from the heart, and this preface should be no different, so let me let you in on a few epiphanies that struck me whilst writing it. Life is hard but exceptional. We mustn't waste it. Do what you love to do, do what's right, and never turn a blind eye to what is wrong, even if it's difficult, because it's not always life that's difficult; more often than not, it's people, and even more so, it's nature. Nature can be ruthless, and it's dangers come in many forms; hurricanes, earthquakes, pandemics, just to name a few. Mother nature is beautiful, but she's a bad bitch. Don't mess with her. Look after the world, and it'll look after you. Life is a double edged diamond blade; cherish it, respect it, and wield it like a sword, or it'll whack you in the head when you least expect it to. We all get whacked in the head sometimes, in one way or another, but we shouldn't blame the world, nor God or Mother nature. If life was perfect, then nothing would be bad. If nothing was bad, then surely nothing would be good, (see how the stars shine bright in the night, but never in day?) so thank your stars when it rains, and hold a

faithful torch through every storm, knowing that
those very stars will keep it lit.
That's pretty lit in itself, I'd say.
Ashley Green

Stained Glass Soldiers

My love for you is a shining star
That sparkles far away
And no matter where you are
I'll love you every day

My love for you is a meadow pure
Of violet flowers sweet
And when you walk on through my door
That's when I feel complete

My love for you is a soldier blue
Your heart I will defend
And I'll always battle on for you
Until the very end

My love for you is the dust of stars
It's a thousand rings of gold
And I'd take a hundred battle scars
To watch us both grow old

My love for you is a stained glass pane
That glistens in the sun
It's a lifelong swing dance in the rain
And it's only just begun

Monsters of the Mind

Be still my friend
In a world of woes,
Let not your passions wilt.
Hold steadfast to the sword of hope;
Hand firmly on the hilt.
And when the doubt comes creeping in
Like ivy down the fence,
Let not those inner monsters win-
They're all but a pretence!

The Artist Adored

I do not miss the playful romance;
For one can't miss what never was.
How would butterflies miss Ellsworth land?
How could Dracula miss Oz?

But I so miss your faithful friendship
And our four at morn guffaws
The memories wait like sitting ducks
Outside our bedroom doors

But where are you now, Juliet?
Do you still laugh and draw?
I still write in the dead of night
Mining words like ore

I heard you have a lover now
And somehow so do I
I dreamt of once, a red haired girl
Now soon, she'll be my bride

Oh will you come to watch us wed,
That gracious special day?
Bring your love, and I'll have mine;
We'll dance the night away

For unrequited love
Is not a magic that we've shared
Oh many songs I've played for you
And many tales you've heard

You grasp the key of friendship
Our love; a now closed door
But friendship never withers
For an artist you adore.

The Valiant Spring

I'm the light on a crisp winter morning
I'm the sea, I'm the Canada sky
I'm the Gingerbread house at the dawning
Where the clouds and the collared doves fly

I'm the lavender lake in the meadow
And the oak where the hummingbirds sing
I'm the candlelit mist by your window
I'm the world; I'm the valiant spring

Gunfire of the Mind

Though life be but a nightmare
With fleeting hours of joy;
An arduous game of truth or dare
With a proneness to destroy-
I keep on walking.

Though love's been but a sacrifice
With fading waves of pleasure
I fell so far to paradise
In hope of finding treasure-
I keep on walking.

Though pain's been but persistent;
A friend that never leaves
I dared remain resistant
To those happiness-stealing thieves-
I keep on walking.

Though my head is but a warzone,
And thoughts; the gunfire of the mind,
It's the best thing that I'll ever own
And I'm proud to say it's mine-
So I keep on walking.

Cerulean Blue

Something draws me back, like the tip of an
arrow
Into endless wastes of sage and yarrow
Where only one sound can be deciphered
Dripping into knowing like oil through the
syphon

So many years have passed since I saw your
eyes
Since we raced down your yard under cerulean
skies
I can still make out the laughter, sometimes the
cries

We were one, so inseparable;
iron and ore
Telling stories of mythics- legends and folklore
But as many lores end, ours was already written
Fate pulled us apart like the okes of a witan

We were somewhere, somehow, lost in
translation
A treasured old Atlas; with no explanation,
discarded, unguarded from thieves and thanes
Withered and weathered by jealousies rains

Cold, freezing wet, I'll never forget
The longing to see you, your dim silhouette
As we lay in the attic
You were the calm one
And I, the fanatic
Drowning in tears, the three musketeers
Dancing our way through those intrepid years
The bad things seemed smaller then, even the fears
But you know what they say about time and fun
You blink and it's over before it's begun

You got a boyfriend and I got depression
It was one heck of a recession
I was knelt on the ground giving breaths and compressions
To the friendship that died.
It was one hell of a ride
You and I,
And that cerulean sky.

The Writer

She asks me, 'why do you write?'
I replied, 'why do we sleep at night?'
Why does the sound glisten under the
moonlight?
Why do birds sing, and why do men fight?

Why do we eat, why on Earth do we drink?
Why do we ponder and why do we think?
Why do we walk, even if we may sink?
Why do we talk, and why do we blink?

Life's a losing game
You can leave, you can stay
You can work your way to fame
You can meditate or pray

But in order to live,
One must bleed, one must fight,
In order to survive,
I must breathe; I must write.

The Coinless Man

Crieth not, the coinless man
For he has borne weights of iron and steel that
others would not dare to touch
Life's trials deflect him
Like hail against stone
Pure and unbreakable, flesh, blood and bone
Undermined by the 'powers,' scorned and sold
short
Climbing desolate towers to get to the good
thoughts
Whilst men of corruption counted their cash
He counted his scars; every smite, every lash
In the silence of night, amidst the promise of day
He listened to what his scars had to say,
Dawn broke; they spoke:
We forged you sir, into the man you are today.

The Poets Painter

The girl that paints her soul onto paper
Little does she know how my soul misses hers
The friendship that kept me alive;
She was the blood when I had none left
She is the only one who can paint the words that
I write
The only one that I could ever trust to

She's walking somewhere in California
Dancing with a brush
Longing for something that is not hers
Or someone – that is not me, for all I know

Be free, be wild, and be you – the best thing you
can be.

Doves of Hope

As the numbers soar
And the souls touch the sky
As loved ones fall and say goodbye
I'll keep you angel in my heart
As we await the worlds new start

And once the reaper bids farewell
And death makes way for spring
We'll remember those who fought and fell
And the old church bells will ring

An eternal song to eulogise
The strength of peace and love
And on that day shall sing and fly
Our heavens holy dove

Night Eternal

Lord be my witness
The world has gone stray
Black ever yonder
And darker by day

Abandoned by our Kings and Courts
They tell us that we're in their thoughts
Yet they snicker whilst we suffer
'Oh the humour of the wrought'

Fickle with their fortunes;
Even more so with their faith
What are we to the richest
But a self-succouring wraith?

Their kids - I've lost count -
Have never gone to bed freezing cold
No, that's a burden for our kids,
Shared by the old

And if that wasn't enough
Now they want war
And when they have that
You can bet they'll want more
Maybe a life, but to keep not to lend,

So tell me now brother, when will it end?

Dawn Everlasting

From the ashes of woe
And the cinders of sorrow
Riseth the dream
Of a brighter tomorrow

Tyranny, SHATTERED
And justice, declared
Freedom, defended
By heavens own fyrd

The wretched have fallen
The worthy have won
An era of unified peace hath begun

Look to tomorrow
But be wise to the past
Now hang up your weapons
And riseth your mast

The church bells of triumph and glory a'blasting
Peace be the key,
To this dawn everlasting

The Lost Vessel of My Body

My soul remains as always
But one day, I will evolve
The world will still be; night and day,
It will surely still revolve.

My eyes; still green as England
My heart; as pure as glass
My touch, as soft as desert sand
This 'phase' will never pass.

Because this is not a phase
And I am destined to be seen
I don't require your approval, nor your praise
For this has always been

In oceans blue and cold reflections
I see myself – a strange perception
Once a vessel lost in sound,
Now finally, I'm found

Timewax

We are all but candles flicking
On a dusty windowsill.
If time is wax, then wax is time that cannot be refilled.

But how your light; so warm and bright
Lights up a thousand rooms
Illuminates the dead of night, and Pharaohs in their tombs

Don't fret about your withered wax,
Nay, smile because you shine
And should your flame grow tired and lame
Relight yourself with mine.

Temple of the Woke

Welcome to the temple of the woke
Where liveth on the whispers of faeries and folk
Worlds apart from the falsehoods of news
Here layeth Gods blueprints, here lie the clues
Untouched by the tainters of fortune and truth
The banes of the different
The sceptics of youth
Blessed air with the savour of myrhh and patchouli
Here lieth the gospel of heaven – yours truly.

Nature's other Mother

Like a ray of sun, you scale the ocean
Surface light and waves of blue sage
Layeth the lores asunder their reflection
Captains emeralds and sapphires blue

Whole cities crumble at the mere sight of her beauty
Jungles burgeon in their place
Bringing forth life, to a new age
This is it
This is us
This is her.

The Orange Garden

I will wisp you away one day
To a glass orange garden in Spain
Where no sound can be heard
But the ditty of birds
And the soft pitter-patter of rain

Dreamchaser

Frail you seem, and scared you are
With eyes of emerald green,
Yet you live, and still you dare
To chase your many dreams
Don't hide away your elegance
Don't give into those fears
Just live your life at your own pace
Don't gallop through the years
For you woke up this morning
That's a blessing in itself
And while the sun was dawning
God promised you good health
So take deep breaths now soldier
There's no need to run away
You're as graceful as a starling
And your heart will lead the way

The Lion and the Alligator

They never did say sorry
For all those times they shut you down
The times they pushed you over-
Turned your planet upside down

They never did say sorry
For the hurtful things they said
And though it many years ago
They still play in your head

They never did say sorry
But you know what? That's okay.
Your enemy will thrash and thwart
Forgive them anyway

They're nothing but a hater
They have nothing nice to say
A vicious alligator
And they thought you were the prey

But what they didn't realise
When they ran their tongue of iron
Was that within that timid heart of yours
Lies the courage of a lion

Of Men and Missiles

Oh ye, of savage men and merciless missiles,
Who do you kneel to, who do you answer to
When dusk has fallen, and only ash and blood
remain?
Do you beg your angels for redemption?
Or is that beyond your comprehension?

Oh How the Nightingale Sings

You may prey on our frail
With your nuclear stings
But oh how the nightingale sings

You can melt down our heirlooms
Our riches and rings
But oh how the nightingale sings

You can try your upmost to destroy everything
Firing your shells at our nightingales wings
But in a meadow not far from your missiles and slings

Still it sings…
  Still it sings…
    Still it sings.

www.ingramcontent.com/pod-product-compliance
Lightning Source LLC
Chambersburg PA
CBHW051755130826
49812CB00033B/1161
9789357699495